THE 28 LAWS OF LISTENING

LISTENING

BEST PRACTICES FOR THE MASTER LISTENER

Dan Oblinger

OTHER WORKS BY
DAN OBLINGER:

Life or Death Listening: A Hostage Negotiator's How-to Guide to Mastering the Essential Communication Skill

Cover designed by Dan Oblinger.

This book is a work of non-fiction. Names, characters, places, and incidents are altered from the author's personal experience to protect the identity of actual people OR are used fictitiously in which case any resemblance to actual persons, living or dead, events, or locales is entirely coincidental.

Please connect with me on LinkedIn at "Dan Oblinger" for additional articles and conversation.

Printed in the United States of America

First Printing: Jan 2019
End of the Drive, Secondhand Ranch, Rose Hill, America

ISBN- 9781793069023

PART ONE

On Law and Listening Well

ON LAW AND LISTENING WELL

A PRIMER

"At his best, man is the noblest of all animals; separated from law and justice, he is the worst."
—*Aristotle*

This short work is a reflection on nearly two decades of public service. It is also the fruit of many years of labor as a consultant for companies who want to add listening and negotiating to their organization's culture. This book incorporates some of the most important lessons from my book, *Life or Death Listening*. I highly recommend it as a comprehensive guide to becoming an authentic listener through emulating the skills used by hostage negotiators. This shorter book you are holding is intended as both an introduction to the deeper, skills-based approach in *Life or Death Listening* and as a refresher or refocusing for those who are well on their way to masterful listening. It should have the effect of applying genuine listening practices to negotiation and leadership strategies in any organization, family, or community. It is also intended to provide a path for building excellent listening habits over four weeks.

The term "law" may seem cold and arbitrary for such an engaging endeavor as listening. As a word associated with public policy or the court system, I agree that "law" is not the ideal way to rule over listening. Instead of thinking of "law" solely as a legal term, consider that laws are truths to be discovered about our world like the law of gravity. Good laws should be moral and natural guides. Proper laws identify what things are and what they are for. Just laws reflect an environment where human beings flourish as they respect these truths.

Laws that govern the critical skill of listening are not my creation. These truths that I call laws are more the product of discovery than invention. They are more like the law of gravity then a speed limit. I propose, as all good laws should, that if you follow these guidelines you will become a masterful listener and serve the good of all.

The life of a master listener is one of inquiry and encounter. Great listeners are needed now more than ever. I pray that this book helps you to be the listener that your organization, community, and family deserves right now. If you consistently adhere to this daily routine, over the course of the next four weeks you will have the opportunity to hone and expand your listening acumen while cultivating a culture of listening at home and work.

Some of the action steps involve other invaluable humans! This is the cultural impact you will need to make a new skill into a habit that is supported by your work environment. Embrace the awkwardness of a new way of doing business as a listener. This is especially challenging since it will change how you communicate with the most important people you know. Carefully consider who you select to assist or join you in this new process of growth and discovery. Pick helpers not hecklers.

I recommended to read no more than one chapter per day. My hope is that you are informed and entertained. More importantly, I pray you will use it to form excellent habits. That is why you should pace yourself and use the full four-week period to digest as you progress. You will find it optimal to maintain a dedicated journal for this listening experiment's daily challenges.

This book, *The 28 Laws of Listening*, is one way to explore this crucial human activity we call listening. If you read one of the 28 laws and wish there were more explanation, it is probably already written in *Life or Death Listening*! I highly recommend having it on hand as you journey through these four weeks of habit formation.

Lastly, these 28 rules for serious listeners echo critical portions of my keynote speeches. If this short book whets your appetite, consider bringing that speech and its constellation of intensive skill-building workshops to an organization in your care. Let us begin...

PART TWO

The 28 Laws of Listening

IT'S NOT ABOUT YOU

THE FIRST LAW

"The poison of selfishness destroys the world."
—Catherine of Siena

Listening is a powerful act of service we do for other people. Listening for hostage negotiators is the ultimate test of empathy. Listening alone without any other helpful activity is a gift we can give to anyone, at any time, and with no cost but our time and attention. Authentic listening is what most people need and want more than anything else. To be done right, you as a listener must offer this service freely and without expectation of return. Your focus must be upon the person you are listening to. Their story is what is essential. When negotiators parlay with criminal suspects or people wrestling with suicidal thoughts, there is a great temptation to violate this law. We, the negotiators, can focus too much on our skill, what we know, what we've accomplished under similar circumstances in the past, and how the incident will affect us.

My first face-to-face negotiation with a jumper presented this temptation. I was worried about two things. One concern was not saying the one thing that might cause her to jump. The second anxiety was in finding the perfect thing to say that would cause her to choose to live. I broke this primary law of listening and negotiating!

It wasn't about me. It was about her. Her emotions, traumas, motivations, fears, beliefs, and values were what got us on top of that building. It was her decision that would get us down safely. What prevented a negotiated surrender from developing at first was her proper perception that I wasn't making it about her. I didn't show her I cared about her perspective by listening deeply to her story.

When my friends, family, co-workers, employees, or clients suspect that the listening session is about me, then all the benefits of listening are diminished. Listening authentically must be empathetic. We must see through the perspective of the other person. We ought to quiet our own emotions and needs so we can detect theirs.

TODAY: Go the entire day without sharing your story. Intentionally and ruthlessly refrain from sharing your thoughts and ideas unless directly invited by someone. Instead, inquire of everyone you can to discover the events of their day, their opinions, and their wellness. Write down any successes or failures. This might be times you would have overshared and didn't or opportunities missed. Continue to do this each day for the rest of the 28-day experience.

LISTENING IS
LIFE OR DEATH

THE SECOND LAW

"Good stories are driven by conflict, tension, and high stakes."
—*William Landay, novelist*

L istening for a hostage negotiator is truly life or death. We work as a team to apply everything we know about empathetic understanding, rapport, and the active listening skills to negotiate a surrender. American police negotiators carry with us stark reminders that the game we play has lethal consequences. While we negotiate, we wear a handgun and body armor. Many times, I have listened intently to a subject's rant while ensconced in an armored car. These physical things remind us of the bottom line. If we do our job properly, people live. If we don't listen well, people could die! This motivates all good police negotiators I've met.

Now consider listening outside the arena of crisis negotiations. We listen to build trust in relationships. Without trust through empathetic listening, the relationship withers. Families, companies, volunteer organizations, and communities are a constellation of human relationships. Listening has monetary implications too! Proper listening is the foundation for sales and client services. Fail to listen to a prospect or client and miss out on a sale. Miss out on too many sales, and the balance sheet turns red. Without proper listening, relationships wither. Income dries up.

Show me your firm's relationships peer to peer, executives to producers, salesforce to prospects, employees to customers. Then I'll know how healthy your company is and how it will fare for the next few quarters. Without listening to each other to seal strong relationships among people, groups drift apart.

The second critical law is that on a long enough timeline, listening is life or death for everyone. Although hostage negotiators know if they succeed at the end of the siege, the effects of your listening skills at work and home take hold over months and years. Choose life!

TODAY: Take stock of the health of your key relationships. Write a list of your most vital human connections at home, at work, and in your life at large. Write their names. Think about the conversations that have become stagnant or one-dimensional. Is it all business? Do you get quality "face-time"? When was the last time you asked someone at work about home or someone at home about their hopes and dreams? Commit to reignite crucial conversations with a few of these VIPs for the rest of this experience.

EVERYONE HAS A STORY

THE THIRD LAW

*"If history were taught in the form of stories, it would
never be forgotten."*
——Rudyard Kipling

Every human being you meet is unique, unrepeatable, irreplaceable, and invaluable. Every good story has a beginning, middle, and end. All of those amazing people in our life have a story to tell. They all come from somewhere, endorse at this present moment a unique combination of cultural influence that informs their present thoughts and feelings, and (this is crucial) have a complex calculus of emotions, desires, values, and beliefs that propel them into the future. I have found this to be true of everyone I have met in my career as a law enforcement officer, hostage negotiator, keynote speaker, and corporate educator.

As a negotiator, I want to know the origin of the crisis, the situation as it exists at the point of crisis, and the intentions and motivations of the actor for resolution of the barricade. Until I've listened deeply enough to discover these aspects of the person's story, we're not ready for a negotiated surrender. Until you, in your leadership role, have listened well enough to know where your employee comes from, where they are in their career and the company culture right now, and where they want to be, you aren't ready to lead either.

Everyone has a rich story of self. Embrace this truth! Obey this law! Rejoice! Since they have this story, they desperately want others to hear the story and find that it is valuable. They might even be selective about whom they share it with. They likely fear rejection. If we invite the story and treat it with respect, we can gain incredible insight into the story's owner and what moves them. The existence of the story is the single greatest opportunity to learn how to be a positive influence the storyteller's life. Remember that we wrap up our self-worth in our story. Respect the story and respect the person. Get busy listening!

TODAY: Without asking them to clarify, write down as much as you remember about your boss's story. Now write out your understanding of the story of your spouse or partner or someone very close to you. Then go listen to them again to rediscover and confirm you truly understand the beginning, middle, and end. How accurate were you? Write down successes and failures. Reflect.

TAKE THE RED PILL

THE FOURTH LAW

"... all I'm offering is the truth."
——*Morpheus,* The Matrix

I n the 1999 movie *The Matrix*, a character named Morpheus, played by Laurence Fishburne, offers the protagonist Neo, played by Keanu Reeves, a choice. He can take the blue pill and his journey ends. Morpheus tells Neo, "You will wake up in your bed and believe what you want to believe".

Or, Morpheus teases, Neo can take the red pill and sees how deep the rabbit hole goes. The blue pill is a blissful status quo. The red pill is the painful and demanding truth. Either way, there is no going back.

Listening is like that. We are already listening all the time. Like the pre-pill Neo in *The Matrix*, most of us are just going through the motions. We are trapped in an illusion. We think we are great listeners and getting the most information and value from our day-to-day conversations with peers and pals. Like Neo, we are increasingly enslaved by a digital overlord that cuts us off from the truth and reprograms us to receive communication that numbs us with contentment. Your smartphone trains your brain to seek pleasure and platitude. Merely "liking" or "sharing" digital content without engaging in meaningful dialogue is not the sort of listening that moves people.

Awakening your mind to the power of great listening will cause you to change at your core. It's going to get messy. You will be aware of your poor listening habits. You will recognize failures of listening in conversations around you at work, home and in the public square. If you really want to be a masterful listener, you're going to find yourself hearing raw stories and receiving terrible news. Listen anyway!

Without creating effective listening environments, you would have been ignorant of these truths. Coworkers, employees, and even your boss may come to you with their traumas. People whose stories (See LAW #3: EVERYONE HAS A STORY) have been bottled up for years without an invitation to share will seize your request and kind ear. Take the red pill and grow closer to your storytellers! After the pain will come the blessings of trust and deeper insight into opportunities around you.

TODAY: Take the red pill. Brace yourself for truths that are unpleasant and stories that are raw and unrehearsed. Start a conversation with someone whose story you have avoided because you know it will hurt. When you are done, write a short review of how this conversation went, what you learned, and how you listened differently. Continue this practice with several of these types of listening partners for the rest of this 28-day experiment.

NEVER MISS A LISTENING OPPORTUNITY

THE FIFTH LAW

"You learn to speak by speaking, to study by studying, to run by running, to work by working, and just so, you learn to love by loving. All those who think to learn in any other way deceive themselves."
—*Francis de Sales*

If you are like me, the last two laws, EVERYONE HAS A STORY and TAKE THE RED PILL get me pumped up! If your eyes have been opened to the importance of listening and the absolute listening deficit that faces most organizations, then you are probably ready to take your listening skill to the next level. What separates the student of listening from the master of listening is the power of listening as a habit.

The eight active listening techniques (see chapters 13-21 in *Life or Death Listening*) are not a magical elixir. You can't carry them with you to be used in an emergency. They are designed to be a tool to improve your natural responses during any conversation. They work best when the listener has used them consistently in all sorts of situations. So where am I going to find all these opportunities for listening?

Get off your couch! Get off your phone! Everywhere and all the time, people present to you an opportunity to listen well. People in waiting rooms, in line at the supermarket, co-workers, and service/hospitality workers. Uber drivers. Once you realize the need for listening and the universe of stories that merely need an invitation from you to begin, the entire world is your listening practice studio. With a kind word and a great question, your next lesson can begin.

One of the best aspects of your listening journey will be seeing people hiding in plain sight. These "grey people" tend to be quiet, unassuming people with amazing stories. Seek them out and invite a listening opportunity.

TODAY: At your office, you have a toilet. Someone cleans it. Find out who it is and have a conversation with them today. Thank them and find out their story! Get on a first name basis. Continue to get on a first-name basis with the people who help you with practice opportunities. (This is one of the most powerful avenues to build trust!) Record success and failures. Continue to practice with those you encounter throughout these 28-days.

LISTEN UNTIL IT HURTS

THE SIXTH LAW

*"When confronted with a situation which we cannot
change, we are then challenged to change ourselves."*
——*Viktor Frankl*

The relationship between listening and problem-solving is intimate. Problem-solving is not the opposite of listening. Most emotional problems require listening as the solution. Even with technical problems, listening should be a big part of the remedy.

When people are emotional about the problem, rushing into problem-solving stifles cooperation and erects new obstacles to a resolution. Problem-solving that is not centered on the good of another person can harm the relationships of the people involved in this process! When our fellow humans are emotional, we will be tempted to ignore their real human need to vent their emotion. Solution-oriented professionals react to stressful conversations and conflict with strategies of problem-solving. We all do this! Under stress, we revert to what we know. We want the comfort of a familiar and orderly process. This is a mistake.

Instead, ask lots of questions about the circumstances and interests that sustain the problem. Allow emotions to subside naturally. Let your partner signal when they are ready for problem-solving to begin. In many cases in my experience, they can solve their problem once you help them calm down through listening to their perspective on the situation. Once you appear to be an ally, they will work with you. Not a minute before!

When we are training police officers to mold them into excellent crisis negotiators, we obey this sixth law- listen until it hurts! That itch of problem-solving strategies wants to be scratched so badly! We repeat this phrase like a mantra, resist the temptation, keep using our listening skills, and embrace the pain of changing our listening habits. Over time, the new negotiator learns that active listening is the most efficient way to solve people problems. Skip listening at your peril! Keep emotions high and watch how ineffective your solutions will be.

TODAY: Look for opportunities to work through problems with people at work and home. Do not dive into solutions. Ask open-ended questions and make non-judgmental observations. Work to relieve emotions without trying to solve anything. Instead, listen until you detect cues that the people facing the problem are ready for problem-solving. Smart police negotiators take their cue from the subject asking the primary negotiator, "What would you do?" or "If you were in my shoes, what would you do?" or the best, "What can we do?" See what happens when you listen until it hurts! Record successes and failures for the rest of the four weeks.

LISTENING MEANS DOING ONLY TWO THINGS AT ONCE

THE SEVENTH LAW

"Simplicity is the ultimate sophistication."
——Leonardo da Vinci

Listening is a powerful and difficult human activity. Listening is also dead simple at its core. There are only two components. You break this natural law of listening when you forget one or the other. Master listeners do two things at the same time when they are on top of their game. This is the time-honored "pat your head and rub your tummy" challenge.

First, listening requires me to be attentive. I must orient myself towards the story. I open my posture, clear my mind, and look at the storyteller. I set aside distractions. Ultimately, the person I am listening to should have a clear sense that I care and that I will give them my full and undivided attention. This must be done without much conscious thought. I should not be distracted by evaluating how attentive I am at any point during the dialogue. It requires practice as recommended in LAW #4: NEVER MISS A LISTENING OPPORTUNITY. Making attentiveness a habit is necessary because of the mental acuity required for the next and greater part of proper listening.

Second, listening requires an appropriate response. This is where many of us fail to be the best listener possible. This failure might manifest through interrupting, one-upping, hijacking the subject, ignoring emotions, or problem-solving too soon. Our active thoughts should focus on receiving the actual message from our partner and considering the best listening tactics to learn more. Instead of listening to respond, we should listen to identify emotions, motivations, values, beliefs, and desires. We listen best when we seek to understand, demonstrate empathy, validate our speaker's worth, and build trust with others.

Fail to be attentive, and the storytelling slows until it stops. Respond inappropriately and risk having fewer opportunities with that important person in the future. Marry them both together and stand back as the magic happens. You are listening masterfully!

TODAY: Practice attentiveness with yourself in the mirror. Then consult with a few trusted colleagues or loved ones. Get their feedback on ways you fail to communicate your attentiveness or fail to respond appropriately to the true messages they have tried to give you I the past. I highly recommend using chapter 6, "Not Listening", in *Life or Death Listening* as a primer. Write about what you learned.

AN OCTOPUS SQUIRTS INK FROM ITS REAR, BUT EMOTIONAL HUMANS ARE STRANGER

THE EIGHTH LAW

"The moment a man talks to his fellows he begins to lie."
—Hilaire Belloc

S orry for this law's long title! It is the favorite part of my keynote on listening culture. It owes its construction to an obscure Oblinger family saying*. My aunt even drew a now infamous epigraph to convey its important message. The defense mechanism of an octopus seems strange, but it is perfectly natural. The ink is just an octopus doing what octopi do!

What is bizarre is a creature that routinely acts against its very nature to its detriment. That creature is *homo sapiens*. It's me and it's you. I owe my long career in American policing to the strangeness of people out of emotional control. The toughest test of active listening is to communicate with people in emotional crisis.

This eighth law represents a real challenge for the budding student of listening. Emotions can be dangerous and frightening. We might wish emotions were not frequently the cause of problems at home and work. Master listeners have learned that the truth of this matter is quite the opposite.

Emotions represent the single greatest opportunity for a seasoned listener. By relieving raw emotions, we gain the trust of a person in distress and thus, become influential in resolving the problem at the center of this emotional crisis. Even positive emotions are listening opportunities. Masterful negotiators use the emotions of every situations to build trust and solve problems.

Human beings are emotional creatures. We always have been and always will be. Learn to recognize and discuss emotions, and you will begin to master the art of gaining rapport through addressing bad, sad, and mad feelings.

TODAY: Write down every human emotion you encounter in your listening opportunities. Every single one. If you label the emotion with the person exhibiting the emotion, record that too! Continue to catalog every emotion for the duration of these 28-days. (I hope you collect them all!) Refer to *Life or Death Listening* chapter 16, "Taming Emotions" for some more insight.

* The original Oblinger family aphorism included the ink and octopus but focused on the strangeness of humans telling lies. I adapted it quickly in my professional career to the broader range of negative human emotions.

SPEAK LESS TO SAY MORE

THE NINTH LAW

"Speak only if it improves upon the silence."
—Mahatma Gandhi

have found that many people are imprecise when describing failures in communication. This can create confusion. As a corporate trainer, I have students report that another key employee is a "terrible communicator" or that two peers "never understand each other". In extreme cases, I've been told by executives that two entire teams within the organization just don't "talk to each other well". I smile because I know what's happening in these cases.

What these cases generally boil down to is a failure in listening. Very few gainfully employed folk have trouble speaking. A bad communicator is usually not failing a test of talking. They are failing in listening which means they are speaking without guidance or context. They are talking at people when they want to speak with people.

This confusion plagues teams when listening is missing from the culture. First, the leader and then the team become isolated through poor listening. When they fail to be attentive or to respond appropriately, fewer and fewer people want to do business with them. This can be both external and internal clients. I call it F.L.I.S. (as in, you've got /fleas/!"), or "Faulty Listening Insulation Syndrome". It often starts at the top of the food chain and then infects the ecosystem downward. Kill, spurn, or frustrate the messenger too many times, and they stop coming to you with their thoughts and ideas.

The remedy is to stop talking so much. Get your listening house in order. Measure your words carefully and make it about the other people and their perspectives. Refer to the previous laws and obey them rigorously when you make the principled decision to open your mouth. Once you have become a habitual and intentional listener, you'll find that you and your team don't need to talk as much as you and they were before. There is a huge benefit on the side. When you are known for high value listening and speaking, your words carry clout. Always start with questions before making pronouncements. Speak up last in a meeting so that everyone hangs on your words. It starts with listening and ends with influence. Isn't it ironic that the best listeners quickly become the sort of speaker that everyone enjoys listening to?

TODAY: Identify a crucial telephone call you will make today. Record it with permission of your calling party. Analyze the amount of time you spoke versus listened. Do this if you can in face-to-face conversations. Strive for 15-25% speaking to 75-85% listening and see what changes in the quality of the information you receive. INFREQUENTLY (2-3 times a week) and with permission, record some critical conversations for the rest of your 28-day habit-building period. Record your progress!

ANYTHING WORTH DOING IS WORTH DOING POORLY

THE TENTH LAW

"Anything worth doing is worth doing poorly."
—*G.K. Chesterton*

There is no such thing as perfect here on Earth. There is no perfect time, there is no perfect place, and I have not found perfect listening yet! The perfect anything is an illusion. Perfection is a mirage. G.K. Chesterton knew this when he wrote out the exact wording of this law approximately 100 years ago.

Sorry to rain on your perfect parade, but it is holding way too many people back. I do not believe there are naturally good listeners and naturally bad listeners and that they cannot improve or decline in skill level. I think everyone has a natural acumen and we can all move up or down this sliding scale of ability. I regularly encounter people who experience my keynotes or participate in my workshops who feel resigned to a life of poor listening. Not so!

The time to start is now. The place to begin is here! There's a meme floating around the internet about a little girl who wanted to be an astronaut. Her mom told her she would have to go to college in engineering, get selected for the astronaut program, and pass the rigorous NASA training. The girl replied nonchalantly, "That's only three things!"

There are also only a few things you need to do to be an excellent listener! It's only slightly more difficult than NASA's process. There are four things. Notice that perfection is absent!

1. You must WANT it.
2. You must convey attentiveness.
3. When people share, respond appropriately.
4. Practice the eight active listening skills and get feedback on the practice.

I consider myself a master listener and have nearly two decades of experience in the field. I am working with the most broken people in society. I also have a decade of private sector experience coaching, training, and educating diverse audiences so they can listen, negotiate, and cultivate cultures that value these activities. Still, I'm not a perfect listener! Far from it. My wife can enlighten you!

I practice every day. Practice is not in a classroom with actors. Practice is with everyone you meet. It is real. I am on a listening journey. Join me. There will be no final state of perfect listening for your journey, but you can be excellent. Start now as a poor listener. It's too important to wait to start until you have improved. Discard perfection and pick up a pen and paper for your challenge today.

TODAY: Write prominently on a piece of paper and post somewhere you spend a lot of time (Car? Desk?) the following: "MY GOAL IS NOT PERFECTION. I WILL BECOME A MASTERFUL LISTENER THROUGH SKILLFUL PRACTICE." That's it. Have a good day!

SMILE!

THE ELEVENTH LAW

"Peace begins with a smile."
—Mother Teresa of Calcutta

How powerful is a smile? My good friend was a homicide detective for many years. He was a talented criminal interrogator. One technique he used was brilliant. He ensured everything was ready to begin an interview with a hardened criminal and then went to Youtube at his desk computer. He played a video featuring the comedic mayhem of Sacha Baron Cohen as "Borat". My friend did this until he was falling out of his chair laughing. Then he would enter the interview room with a genuine smile. This sort of genuine smile disarms a murderer facing his crime.

Smiles for listeners are also disarming. A smile is a powerful message that you enjoy the story you are receiving and want to know more. Smiles telegraph joy. A smile changes your face and voice. Hostage negotiators do most of our work by phone, and we know that our subjects can detect the sound of a smile in our voice.

Joy is a necessary attribute of excellent listeners and leaders. Joy is infectious. I believe that becoming excellent at some skill is much easier when there is joy in the work. Joy is a proper understanding that we are all so richly blessed to be living here and now. Everything we have is a gift. Joy is a protection against the sort of bland attitude that sinks trust relationships and ends influence. People want to do business with happy people. People look at joy as proof of competence and expertise. A smile on the face is an obvious and convincing proof of joy in the soul. That is why it is smart to follow this law. Smile when you engage in authentic listening!

TODAY: Write down your top ten blessings so you will have ten reasons to smile today as you listen to others!

RESPECT THE FEEL-THINK-DO CONNECTION

THE TWELFTH LAW

"There comes a time when all the cosmic tumblers have clicked into place- and the universe opens itself up for a few seconds to show you what's possible."
—Ray Kinsella quoting Terence Mann, Field of Dreams

This law of listening is useful for helping people in crisis or when performance suffers. We know that we all have feelings. We also understand that we have thoughts that are distinct from feelings. Besides our thoughts and feelings, we also have actions. Actions are not feelings or thoughts. What we might fail to appreciate is the connection between these three areas of existence. How I feel impacts my thoughts. What I think and what I feel impel my actions.

This law comes straight from the school of Cognitive Behavioral Therapy in modern psychology. It functions like a triangle, not a flow chart. If one corner of this feeling-thinking-doing construction goes wrong, it impacts the other two corners. If I feel bad, I often think bad. Bad thoughts and foul mood lead to bad decisions and behavior. Acting badly can feed back into more bad thoughts and ill feelings. One dark thought can worsen our mood and behavior.

Fortunately, this law also governs good feelings, positive thoughts, and upright actions. Improve one and potentially change them all for the better. More relevant for our goal with this law, listening well is a reliable and repeatable method to improve someone's mood and help them think more clearly. Instead of making them act better, through empathy and trust we can help them naturally improve their behavior. This is a subtle, but important distinction for managers and leaders. By working within the triangle of feelings, thoughts, and actions you can persuade and influence without resorting to sheer authority. This opens the possibility of leading through the consent of those you lead. This is better for the health of your culture. In engenders trust and internal motivation on your team.

Once you become adept at intervening in this model, the universe of people will open like Ray Kinsella's cosmic tumblers. Go the distance!

TODAY: Write down a few behaviors on your team or in your home that are problematic. Now make educated guesses about the thoughts or feelings tied to the actions of concern. If necessary, have conversations with those involved to confirm or clarify. Begin to make a habit of looking for the missing corners of the triangle when a bad feeling, thought, or action appears.

IF YOU ARE TOO BUSY TO LISTEN, YOU ARE TOO BUSY

THE THIRTEENTH LAW

"It's a twap!"
——Fleet Admiral Ackbar, Rebel Alliance, Star Wars
Episode IV: Return of the Jedi

I was walking into work and the Chief Executive of my organization was walking out. He caught me and said something that you may have heard before. Perhaps like me, you've said it before! He said, "I need more time with you." His sentiment was genuine, but the thinking was problematic. We don't manufacture time.

One of most frequent and fervent objections I hear in my listening seminars comes from executives and upper management. They ask where they will find the time to listen in the way I advocate- deeply, patiently, and authentically. I ask them where they find the time to NOT listen well! When we don't listen, we make mistakes, lose the respect of our team, and miss out on opportunities. These opportunities are often efficiencies in time, effort, and quality of output. Listening isn't the fastest way to solve problems or build up teams. It is the most efficient.

I have come to realize as a leader that our belief that we are controlled by time, in the words of Admiral Ackbar, is a "twap"! We get sucked into the daily grind and a mountain of tasks. It is easy to lose sight of the people who will accomplish the work for us. Show me your schedule and I'll see your values. If you jam-pack your day with meetings and events, you will leave no time for the listening opportunities that present themselves through the course of your day.

I have found the greatest benefit to my relationships by seizing these spontaneous opportunities to listen deeply without the pressure of the next three things on my calendar. This law reflects a universal truth of leadership and management. If you are too busy to listen, then you are just too busy. Make a change.

TODAY: Reorganize your schedule. Build in a few 15-minute blocks for listening. You can plan some conversations or build in buffers between activities or meetings to take advantage of spontaneous listening opportunities.

BUILD MORE CAMPFIRES

THE FOURTEENTH LAW

*"The echoes of beauty you've seen transpire, Resound
through dying coals of a campfire."*
—Ernest Hemingway

Listening never occurs in a vacuum. Smart listeners create environments where people tell stories. A huge bonfire is a dramatic image for me living in the middle of a vast prairie. Around the campfire ring, stories are freely told. What makes campfires great is that we can talk about anything. There is something about a campfire's light and warmth that creates trust and shakes good stories free from the tellers.

The campfire listening experience can happen indoors too! By practicing good listening habits, we can create listening environments anywhere. If we don't, we will be working in a company where many important topics are off limits because people are afraid to discuss them. Leaders miss out when they fail to shape the listening environment and coax these tough conversations from their team. Everyone should have a clear sense that they can talk about anything for the good of the team, community, or family. If not, we have work to do.

Our bad listening habits extinguish the fires that inspire stories. Interrupt or one-up your story teller, and you have destroyed the campfire atmosphere. Imagine the effect on future listening opportunities when you create the impression that their story is not important.

Good listeners are intentional with the setting for listening. A place that allows us to hear clearly and minimizes distractions is ideal. A small group can listen to each other and share ideas. Larger groups require one-way communications and offer limited feedback. In-person meetings have definite advantages. Phone conferences are a scourge. Text messages have a narrow but useful application. That raises the issue of social media.

Our use of the digital communications environment does not mean that listening is dead. Although digital devices and social media make listening a challenge, we can still create valuable dialogue. Instead of clicking on a button to "Like" or "Share", send a message to the content creator and ask profound questions! There is a real possibility to light a virtual campfire if you engage people properly. Again, a private message is more likely to start something valuable than a public post open to the trolls!

It only takes one intentional listener to create an environment where a storyteller feels safe. Campfires need not be fancy or complicated to create something from nothing. One habit I have is to respond to socially trite questions in unique and inviting ways. How many times has someone in public asked you, "How are you?" or "How's your day going?" Develop a response that is positive and upbeat and invites a genuine response. Steal mine: "I'm blessed!" I have initiated more listening opportunities with those two words than any others. Get some kindling and start something good!

TODAY: Instead of "liking", "retweeting", or "reacting" to social media posts today, try to start three conversations on social media with content creators. Give them quality feedback or ask for more information on the subject at hand. In real life, give your team permission to tell you anything they need for the good of the organization. Be prepared when they take you up on the offer!

IF YOU HAVEN'T ASKED, YOU DON'T KNOW

THE FIFTEENTH LAW

"It is error only, and not truth, that shrinks from inquiry."
——Thomas Paine

One of the important applications of listening skills for the budding leader-listener is to ask the questions that solicit the real story. This is a combination of attentiveness in asking the right question and selling your sincere desire to have the truth. This requires the truth holder to believe upon experience and reputation that if he or she gives you their honest appraisal that you will react appropriately. This means with gratitude and discretion!

Leaders should be knowledge brokers. We ought to know our reputation as leaders, the reputation of our key employees among peers, the health of our brand in our industry and the broader marketplace. In all but the most cultivated corporate listening cultures, this sort of vital information will not be volunteered. One major failing of leaders at every level of every organization is to assume that our teams or clients will bring us the information we need about ourselves and our companies to make critical decisions. We are constantly tempted to fill these gaps in our knowledge with assumptions or hopes. This is not good listening or leadership.

Ultimately, I have found that in our listening life I get what we invite, not what people volunteer. Smartly constructed questions, insightful reflection, and respecting the first law of listening (IT'S NOT ABOUT YOU) will yield valuable insight into your culture and people.

TODAY: Go ask a trusted colleague what your reputation is as a leader in your organization. Be sincere. Be humble. Thank them for the courage when they tell you something you dislike. Respond appropriately. Record the results. Repeat this as needed over the next few weeks to discover amazing things about yourself, your team, and your firm.

BE COVERT

THE SIXTEENTH LAW

"Short cuts make for long delays."
—*Peregrine "Pippin" Took, J.R.R. Tolkien's* The
Fellowship of the Ring

Actively listening to another person is a covert activity. It is subtle. It is not flashy. It should cause reflection in our communication partners rather than suspicion. It focuses on the other person to discover what they know. At the same time, listening is not data extraction. The goal is not to "get information from people". The goal is to build a relationship of trust. One by-product of this trust is information. People we trust have a wealth of information about us.

Work to make listening techniques natural. You should deliver questions with your unique style. For this reason, crisis negotiators don't script out anything. We respond to what is said. We improvise and adapt to the story as it unfolds. Our intelligence gathering is restricted to what the person feels comfortable disclosing instead of pushing for their story on my terms and inviting deception. In this way, I always get more insight and knowledge from people through mutual trust.

TODAY: Start up a conversation with a total stranger. See how much insight you can gain into their life without asking direct questions. Simply use good listening techniques to demonstrate empathy and build trust.   Record success or failures.

TRUST IS THE CURRENCY OF LISTENING

THE SEVENTEENTH LAW

*"The friend in my adversity I shall always cherish most.
I can better trust those who helped to relieve the gloom
of my dark hours than those who are so ready to enjoy
with me the sunshine of my prosperity."*
—*Ulysses S. Grant*

Listening is not the end-state for relationships and teamwork. Listening is the foundation for accomplishing hard work with other people. With a firm commitment to listening as a habit, we build trust with anyone who will share their story. This starts with turning listening skills into listening habits. A firm commitment to listening demonstrates empathy and builds mutual trust over time. I have found that this trust what we can use to ask others to take risks with us to accomplish great things. I often earn the trust of a suspect to ask them to give up a dangerous plan.

Our goal in listening need not be to merely listen, listen, and listen some more. As a negotiator, I would not be very skillful or successful if all I do is listen. My listening has purpose. It should generate trust. Trust is earned. What we might forget as leaders is that trust must also be spent. Trust, also called rapport in my industry, is spent wisely to move people to feel, think, or act better. This is the core function of leadership.

Use listening to earn trust as a leader. It works like precious currency, and currency exists to be spent. If I don't listen well to gain trust before I ask my team to do something risky or difficult, they will rebel. It is like being overdrawn on your checking account! There's no currency there to spend.

With authentic listening up front, I have emotional trust funds to spend on tough tasks. Listen well to gain enough respect from your followers, and you can accomplish amazing things!

TODAY: Consider who you ask to do the most at work or around the house. We all have high performers who do the lion's share of the work. Go have a high-quality conversation with them to deposit currency in the account. Don't ask them to do anything for you or the team today. Just listen.

GET A DAILY DOSE OF SILENCE

THE EIGHTEENTH LAW

"If he is not edified by my silence, he will not be edified by my speech."
—Abba Pambo, Desert Father (c. 2nd Century Christianity)

We live in a world of noise. Many of us are on digital devices most of the day. It is titillating! We consume an enormous quantity of digital content. It is almost a constant activity. Most of us check our phones before we even get out of bed. Some of us leave a streaming audio service or movie running as we fall asleep. There's a big problem. The human mind is not made for constant stimulation!

To truly progress as a master listener, you will need introspection. There is a real connection between regular, intentional silence and proper listening habits. One of the active listening skills is the use of silence to build a conversation (*Life or Death Listening,* Ch. 17 "Sometimes Say Nothing"). To do this properly and to accurately take stock of your progress, build silence into your day.

TODAY: Find 30 minutes every day for intentional silence. This means no human or digital interaction. Find a quiet place to just be alone with your thoughts. Anticipate that this will be challenging at first. Over time, this period of silence will become more valuable as you become accustomed to silence and the healthy benefits of organizing your thoughts and taking stock of your emotional health. I highly recommend journaling during this period. Sometimes in a pinch, I use my commute. I drive and think without a radio, phone calls, or passengers. Try it! Then, increase it.

AGREE

THE NINETEENTH LAW

"When people are divided, the only solution is agreement."
—John Hume

istening seems easy until you need to listen to a person you dislike! As a professional negotiator, I do not have the luxury of picking my listening opportunities. I serve a most disagreeable population of clients. Despite this, conflict is my favorite! Police negotiators have learned a simple technique for starting our listening sessions with a positive boost. The best part is that this amazing tactic only needs two words.

The powerful phrase that disarms conflict and opens the minds of others to your influence is "I agree." Even if you must qualify the precise limits of this agreement, merely saying these words is a game-changer. "I agree" says so much. It says, "you are right about THIS", "we can work together", "I am being reasonable", "I am listening", and "I want to help".

"I agree" consistently moves the other person to reciprocate your agreeable demeanor. They will find areas of agreement. Sometimes this must be through concession. Now a negotiation has begun in earnest! In the face of obvious disagreement and conflict, agreeing with someone who is emotional quickly takes the proverbial wind from their negative emotion's sails. It sets the tone for listening and mutual respect.

TODAY: Use "I agree" as often as possible when it is true! Record each instance that it opens a conversation or generates a concession. Keep doing this.

SHOW, DON'T TELL

THE TWENTIETH LAW

"They do not love who do not show their love."
—*William Shakespeare*

This law is simple. The most important messages we send are "I am listening", "I understand", "I will be there for you", and "you can trust me". Especially for our family and dear friends, there is no greater phrase than "I love you". The worst way to convey these important sentiments is to say them directly.

We strictly instruct new negotiators to avoid saying these phrases. It takes time for an untrained communicator to let go of these crutches. Crutches is precisely what they are! Especially in a crisis state, the person we are listening to could react negatively to these reassurances if we haven't backed them up with our actions and listening acumen.

Using the active listening techniques, there are a myriad of ways to demonstrate that you are listening and understanding someone else. You show them you are listening by paraphrasing or summarizing the main ideas, labelling the key emotion, or making an insight that was expressed but unstated. We show we care, support, and can be trusted by being attentive and responding appropriately. For our family, we show them we love them by acts of service and self-sacrifice. Authentic listening is an act of love. The words are nice, but people will believe it when we show them.

TODAY: Strike the crutch phrases from your vocabulary. Be an artful listener and show others you are listening through your skill!

LISTENING ENGAGES EVERYONE

THE TWENTY-FIRST LAW

"We all think we are connected to the world now, but we are not talking to our neighbours anymore."
——Jean-Michel Jarre

We crave human connection, validation of our impassioned work, and positive feedback for accomplishments. We need to believe that we are indispensable and have a bright future with our organization.

As a keynote speaker, I was recently asked about "millennials". I can be a light-hearted speaker, but the questioner was quite serious. I could tell he had a specific employee on his mind. I get asked frequently about diversity as it relates to listening and negotiating. Here's my answer with a small caveat first- *if you are working with a human being who is capable of rational thought and communication,* you should listen to everyone authentically to find out the best way to manage them!

Everyone is a unique and beautiful butterfly. Your generational placement influences your perspective. Where you grew up and who raised you matters. Demographics can be insightful. Fortunately, the best way to attend to everyone is through great listening. Even millennials!

Stop putting people in categories. If you want to engage your employees, listen to them individually. If you want to determine what motivates them, listen to each of them individually and ask! If you want to improve retention and talent acquisition, make intentional listening a core element of your work culture. Same for families. Listen well to hold it together!

TODAY: Begin, if you haven't yet, a longitudinal conversation with all your direct reports and your direct supervisor about expectations and preferred ways to communicate at work. Longitudinal conversations mean we intend to talk about this issue and continue talking about it periodically and perpetually because the topic is so important and constantly evolving.

INQUIRY OVER ADVOCACY

THE TWENTY-SECOND LAW

"Well, how's that working out for you?"
— Dr. Phil

Leaders attempting to listen can adopt only one of two spirits. There is the spirit of advocacy. This means knowing the answer and leading the employee to this truth. The other is a spirit of inquiry. This is a genuine desire to know what the employee knows and to discover how and why they formed that impression. These are questions that do not supply the answer.

This law is a gentle reminder to leaders that the spirit of inquiry is superior at building a culture of trust, engagement, and productivity. There is a place for advocacy in leadership. It is best used after the difficult listening is done and we know the best way to persuade the employee. Dr. Phil is a marvelous TV personality, but when he asks his infamous question "How's that working out for you?" it is advocacy. He knows how it is working out: not well. Instead, be an inquirer.

This is a fine place to point out one of the critical abilities that separates bad negotiators from the fantastic. Selling this spirit of inquiry falls largely on the use of the voice as a versatile tool. We create this inquisitive vibe through our tone of empathy and a desire to understand. We can also clearly indicate that we know the answer to our own question with a tone of sarcasm, authority, or arrogance. Know the difference and never mix up these signals!

TODAY: Ask before you tell. Don't decide anything or instruct anyone until you clearly know what is happening or where they stand on the issue in question. Write down any instances where you think you advocated instead of inquired.

LISTENING HEALS LONELINESS

THE TWENTY-THIRD LAW

"We have all known the long loneliness, and we have found the answer is community."
—*Dorothy Day*

We live in the most technologically advanced civilization in the history of the world. We have more ways to communicate with each other and with nearly everyone in the world than anyone who came before us. We are at the pinnacle of communication technology. And we are at the same time the saddest and most pitiable of peoples.

Our society's general depression can now be defined as a form of loneliness. We can be on a crowded train or bus, see on social media that we were not invited to a party, and feel immensely lonely. Many people in New York City report being lonely despite living in 300 square miles with 8.6 million other folks!

You should take this as a challenge. No one should have to be lonely, provided people would just listen to them! Listening is the antidote to the loneliness disease. This disease is a pandemic. It kills. Listening can help fight depression and suicide.

Listening to fight loneliness is about encounter and invitation. Seek out those who are on the margins of your culture. Light a campfire, ask some compelling questions, and begin a conversation. These sorts of conversations are what pull colleagues together to form a healthier corporate body. They nourish the lives of families.

Here's the best part. Properly understood, listening heals the listener too. Community means we all get better together. The life you save might be your own!

TODAY: Make a public post to your social media accounts offering to listen to anyone who feels lonely and wants to talk offline or through direct message. Digital media can be used for good! See what happens. Record your thoughts.

LET THE ELEPHANTS OUT OF THE ROOM

THE TWENTY-FOURTH LAW

"Anything that's human is mentionable, and anything that is mentionable can be more manageable. When we can talk about our feelings, they become less overwhelming, less upsetting, and less scary. The people we trust with that important talk can help us know we are not alone."
—Mister Fred Rogers

Make everything safe to discuss. Freeing a team to talk about performance, obstacles, and opportunities works like a fresh breeze to air out your corporate culture. Talking about complicated issues and historical trauma is a healthy practice for a family.

When you recognize a topic that must be discussed, immediately dive in using active listening skills. Listening in the way I recommend allows you to discuss anything with anyone. The reason is that you are seeking the other person's opinion, perspective, or knowledge of this important subject. Everyone's favorite subject is himself or herself! Approaching any difficult conversation with a genuine inquiry is likely to succeed.

There is a great danger in avoiding crucial conversations. Room elephants tend to gather in herds. Leave things unsaid and problems unearthed, and they multiply. Let them out using a spirit of inquiry and the eight active listening skills.

TODAY: Ask several influential people at work about topics they think are taboo. Discuss those sensitive subjects. Explore why they formed the opinion that the discussions were off-limits.

GIVE UNCONDITIONAL POSITIVE REGARD

THE TWENTY-FIFTH LAW

"The kind of caring that the client-centered therapist desires to achieve is a gullible caring, in which clients are accepted as they say they are, not with a lurking suspicion in the therapist's mind that they may, in fact, be otherwise. This attitude is not stupidity on the therapist's part; it is the kind of attitude that is most likely to lead to trust."
— Dr. Carl R. Rogers

As your listening skill improves, you will find yourself in deeper conversational waters. Keep this law in mind. No matter what people tell you, be grateful. Offer warm, positive regard to their perspective. Do not put conditions upon the sentiments or thoughts they offer you. If we invalidate the emotions or thoughts of our storytellers, we fail them and stifle the listening process.

Dr. Carl Rogers pioneered this concept for therapists. It works on the street. Do not pass your judgment when people are courageously sharing. As a police negotiator, I often speak with people who have done unspeakable horrors. We listen with this same Rogerian regard. It's our duty. We are bound to keep this channel of information and persuasion open. We don't have the luxury of passing moral judgment when lives are at stake.

I highly recommend you do the same. Listen without forming a judgment at work and in your home. There will be time for gentle moral correction later. For now, meet people where they are and invite them to share.

TODAY: Think back to a conversation where your disdain for the person, their actions, or their beliefs caused the conversation to sour. Script out how you might listen differently with this law in mind. If possible, find the person today and revisit this issue. Begin with an apology and strive to be vulnerable. For more background, research Dr. Carl Rogers's work.

CHANGE YOURSELF & INFLUENCE OTHERS

THE TWENTY-SIXTH LAW

"Everyone thinks of changing the world, but no one thinks of changing himself."
— Leo Tolstoy

L istening well places demands on us as listeners. We must make some changes. Changing habits is hard. These 28-days represent a good start! Listening is made more difficult because we are working with other people that might also need to change.

Recall the first law of listening, IT'S NOT ABOUT YOU. That law referred to the person who should be in control of the story and receive the listening focus. This is a corollary. The decision to jump is the person who is threatening to jump! The decision to listen better every day is yours. Know what you can control.

Respect this law of listening to have a more peaceful existence. You are only responsible for your attitude and efforts to change through forming positive habits. You cannot make people become better. Through listening, empathy, and building a relationship of trust you can have enormous influence to persuade others to change. This is an entirely different process than cajoling, demanding, or threatening others to make changes in habit. Persuasion and influence are deft, subtle approaches that are proven to work. Trying to change other people without their permission or cooperation leads to frustration. Frustration leads to quitting. Never quit. Change your own habits to better serve all.

TODAY: Continue the practices from the previous laws. Commit to not trying to change people without their cooperation.

T.W.W.D.I.O.I.T.W.W.D.I.O.

THE TWENTY-SEVENTH LAW

"That which we despise in others is that which we despise in ourselves."
—Sign on Fr. Tom Jennings's door, IHM Seminary (c. 2000 A.D.)

As you grow in listening ability, you will become acutely aware of the listening failures around you. None of these will be more apparent than the people who mean the most in your life. People will be unreasonable. Listen to them, love them, and lead them anyway. Be humble in your skill. Humility is a secret ingredient in listening well. Be vulnerable. Otherwise, you will not be able to develop relationships of trust and potential storytellers will not find you approachable.

Before I was a hostage negotiator, keynote speaker, author, or even a beat cop, I studied to be a Roman Catholic priest. On the door of the Vice Rector's office hung a sign that I will never forget. It said, "That Which We Despise in Others is That Which We Despise in Ourselves."

Anytime you recognize some fault in another person, especially in their listening habits, remember Father Jennings's sign! The reason you see that imperfection is because you've seen it before in yourself. We are most attuned to the human frailties that we struggle with internally. This law will keep you grounded and empathetic. These are two essential qualities of a master listener.

TODAY: Recognize a poor listening habit in someone else and be kind. Ask them if you can offer a suggestion. This is hard, I know! With their permission, simply make an observation- "I noticed that...", describe the deficiency without making it personal, and offer a simple suggestion for improvement. Once you've done that, your work is done. The rest is up to them!)

ASSEMBLE A TRIBE

THE TWENTY-EIGHTH LAW

*"Individual commitment to a group effort – that is what
makes a team work, a company work, a society work,
and a civilization work."*
—*Vince Lombardi*

This is the end of your master listening kick-start. You committed to becoming an intentional and intelligent listener. You have accepted the central role of listening in leading and loving others genuinely. I hope you have become a student of the eight active listening skills! I pray you will continue to practice them. They are the only way I've found to improve the natural way you respond to the stories of those around you. You should be able to recognize and embrace listening opportunities. Now a hard question comes. By making these intense and difficult personal changes, how much have you changed your organization?

Culture resists designed change. Since organizational culture is constructed of such a complex blend of influences from a multitude of people, it is nearly impervious to the desired change of a single person. This is true even if that person is the "boss"!

If you want to change your culture, you'll need a team. A group, even a small cohort, with a common language, skillset, and purpose can have a tremendous impact on culture. If you want to add listening to a culture, you will need to add two, three, or more master listeners. You will need the encouragement, feedback, and accountability that only your listening tribe can offer.

TODAY: Find those people who are primed to improve their listening game. Give them this book. Introduce them to your plan for adding intentional listening to the broader corporate culture. Challenge them to change themselves and influence others! Let me know how it goes...

NOW WHAT?

WHAT IS THE NEXT BIG THING? If you found value in this book and its 28 lessons in listening, then do not stop now! If you want to know more about authentic listening culture and all eight active listening skills that hostage negotiators use to create consensus and save lives, then consider reading my book, *Life or Death Listening* available on Amazon.com as a Kindle eBook and in paperback. If you want something more challenging, contact me to find out more about my seminars and workshops for skills-based training, and keynote speaking for building a culture of listening wherever you need it! Please give a 5-star review on Amazon. If you didn't get 5-star value, contact me at dan.oblinger@gmail.com so I can learn from you what needs improvement. Connect with me on LinkedIn to stay current on educational opportunities and funny listening stories! It's free and it cannot hurt!

ABOUT THE AUTHOR

DAN OBLINGER IS A UNIQUE VOICE IN CORPORATE TRAINING AND KEYNOTES. He is a father, husband, philosopher, and lawman. Oblinger has been successful in his professional life as a hostage negotiator, undercover human trafficking investigator, chicken rancher, drug recognition expert, human resources consultant, ditch digger, landlord, grocery bagger, onion ring maker, small business owner, and beat cop. Dan's total ownership of culture as the commander of several elite units of investigators and negotiators informs his belief in what he teaches. He has used his unique experiences and high energy humor to educate audiences across America since 2008. Dan has carved out a niche as a leading expert in providing speaking, training, and executive consulting for diverse industries and client firms. Dan's passion is sharing listening, negotiating, and leadership skills so everyone can become more authentic leaders and lovers. His message is simple and refreshing: Listen well and negotiate for consensus to cultivate excellence in corporate culture. Everyone has an amazing story to tell, and it is our job to invite them to tell it!

Want to have him speak at your conference or train your key people? You can reach him on LinkedIn, or by email at dan.oblinger@gmail.com.

Dan lives happily with his wife and five adopted children on a small homestead in rural Kansas. *Ad Astra Per Aspera!*

Made in the USA
Columbia, SC
17 November 2024